295

LITTLE
CRAFT BOOK
SERIES

needlepoint simplified

By
Jo Ippolito Christensen
and
Sonie Shapiro Ashner

photographs by Mike E. Bergen

STERLING
PUBLISHING CO., INC. NEW YORK
SAUNDERS OF TORONTO, Ltd., Don Mills, Canada

Oak Tree Press Co., Ltd.
London & Sydney

Little Craft Book Series

Dedicated to our very patient husbands, Captain John J. Christensen, USAF, and Louis Ashner.

The authors would like to thank Sonie Ashner's mother and partner in Morningside Knit Shop, Kansas City, Missouri, Mrs. Dorothy Shapiro Amdur, for inspiration.

Projects on pages 7 and 10 appear courtesy of John Dritz and Sons. Chart of Siamese cat (page 33) is adapted and reprinted by permission of Charles Scribner's Sons and Faber and Faber, Ltd. from NEEDLEPOINT, page 47, by Hope Hanley. Copyright © 1964 by Hope Hanley. Doorstop on page 35 stitched by Len Kelly. Lion and tiger pillows on page 43 stitched by Louise Mayer. Picture on page 31 stitched by Mrs. Sylvia Lieberman.

Drawings by Susan Henderson

Copyright © 1971 by Sterling Publishing Co., Inc.
419 Park Avenue South, New York, N.Y. 10016
Simultaneously published and Copyright © 1971 in Canada
by Saunders of Toronto, Ltd., Don Mills, Ontario
British edition published by Oak Tree Press Co., Ltd., Nassau, Bahamas
Distributed in Australia by Oak Tree Press Co., Ltd.,
P.O. Box 34, Brickfield Hill, Sydney 2000, N.S.W.
Distributed in the United Kingdom and elsewhere in the British Commonwealth
by Ward Lock Ltd., 116 Baker Street, London W 1
Manufactured in the United States of America
All rights reserved
Library of Congress Catalog Card No.: 75-167666
ISBN 0-8069-5178-8   UK 7061 2322 0
5179-6

Contents

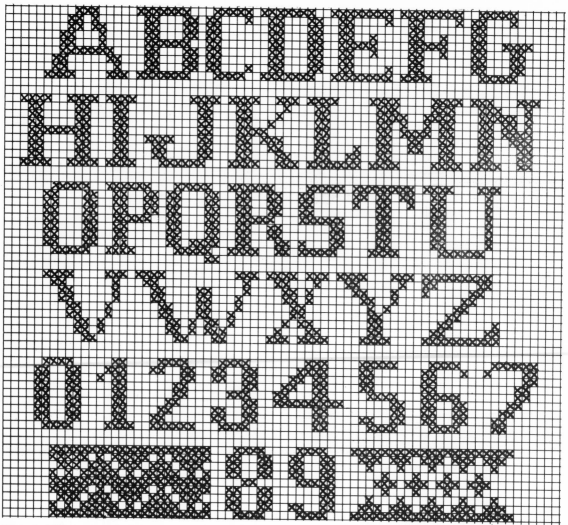

Illus. 1. When you stitch letters and numbers in needlepoint, use the Continental stitch (page 7). Each "x" in the diagram here counts as one stitch. If you accidently stitch an area or a letter incorrectly, carefully snip each stitch with embroidery scissors and pull the yarn out with tweezers. If this leaves a weak spot in the canvas, baste a new piece right under the weak area; then do needlepoint as usual.

4

Before You Begin

Ladies of leisure used to while away their time by stitching delicate needlepoint accessories. Life is more hectic today, what with appointments, meetings, and errands—but we do occasionally have some spare time. Needlepoint is still a worthwhile and enjoyable pastime during those random hours. A needlepoint revival began in the 1960's, when manufacturers introduced bright new yarns and lively designs on canvas. Today's woman is discovering this ageless craft and enhancing her modern home with its patterns.

Needlepoint is embroidery on a canvas background. There are three basic kinds of stitches—horizontal, vertical and diagonal—and a limitless number of colors. The designs that can be made by combining different stitches and colors are virtually endless. The items on the following list have one thing in common—they can all be decorated with needlepoint! Try your hand at one of these: slippers, man's vest, bolero, suspenders, belt, headband, choker, coat, eyeglass case, wallet, purse, tote bag, tennis racket cover, cosmetic bag, initials on a purse, pillow, book cover, wall hanging, curtain tie backs, doorstop, footstool or bench cover, upholstered chairs, rug, card table cover, pin cushion, or picture.

Materials

The canvas you choose for the background largely determines the appearance of your finished needlepoint—rugged, on a canvas with few mesh per inch, or dainty, on a tightly woven canvas. Most needlepoint is done on Penelope 10 (10 mesh to the inch), but for stitches which cover canvas densely, use a looser canvas, and for stitches which do not cover well, use a tighter canvas. Canvas comes in two styles, Penelope and Mono (also called Congress). Mono is woven with a single thread, while Penelope is woven in pairs of threads. Generally, vertical stitches are used on Mono, and diagonal ones on Penelope, for best coverage.

You can buy canvas by the yard the same way you buy fabric, and then plan and stitch an original design. Or buy a needlepoint kit with the design stamped on the canvas, sometimes even with the more intricate sections already stitched. These kits cost a little more than plain canvas and yarn, but you are not paying for the materials alone: the

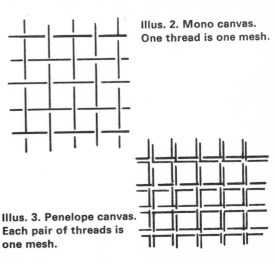

Illus. 2. Mono canvas. One thread is one mesh.

Illus. 3. Penelope canvas. Each pair of threads is one mesh.

price includes the carefully planned design and choice of colors. These kits allow you to practice different stitches in an appropriate design.

The blunt end tapestry needle you use should be narrow enough to fall through the holes in the canvas easily, while the eye of the needle must be large enough for the yarn. HINT: To thread the needle easily, flatten the yarn between the fattest part of thumb and index finger. Do not wet the yarn. Push the needle through your fingers and the needle will be threaded.

Express yourself in needlepoint the way an artist expresses himself in painting, with colors and textures to complement your design. Needlepoint is not difficult, and it should not become a chore. Pick colors and patterns that please you, relax with everything you need nearby, and enjoy your stitching!

Illus. 4. Personalize a needlepoint handbag by spelling out your initials or your name. Always use tapestry yarn for needlepoint: it is mothproofed, comes in matched dye lots and has long, strong fibres. Because it is 4-ply, you can split strands for thinner or thicker yarn.

Owl and Mushroom Doorstop

Stitching

You can buy a needlepoint canvas with the design already worked, on which you fill in just the background. These canvases are designed by skilled craftsmen who are familiar with the suitability of a pattern for needlepoint, and who can determine the most pleasing designs and colors. When you are more skilled with needlepoint, design your own pattern—but while you are practicing the stitches, a canvas that is already stamped or partially stitched is a great learning aid!

The doorstop in Illus. 53 is actually a brick covered with needlepoint canvas. The canvas was purchased with the owl and mushroom motif already completed and just the background to be filled in with any color and stitch. The following are some background stitches most commonly used:

Continental stitch: Also called the *Tent stitch*, this is the most common of background possibilities. Bring the needle, threaded with an 18″-piece of yarn, from the wrong side to the right side through one hole about 2″ from the edge of the canvas, and pull the yarn until about 1″ remains on the wrong side. As you stitch, work over this end to hold it in place. This is the way to start all new threads in needlepoint.

Insert the needle to the wrong side through the hole above and to the right of the first one, then to the right side through the hole to the left of the first one. Pull the yarn evenly but not tightly. Work an entire row; then turn the canvas so you work in the same direction for the second row. To end a thread, run it through several stitches on the wrong side of the piece. There should be no knots in needlepoint. The Continental stitch uses a lot of yarn for a small area, because it covers both the front and back of the canvas. A piece done with this stitch can therefore take much wear.

Half Cross stitch: This stitch looks like the Continental on the right side, but it is made differently and does not cover the back of the canvas well. Use it on articles that receive little wear—pictures or wall hangings, for example.

Begin stitching in a hole at the upper left corner of the canvas. Insert the needle to the wrong side of the canvas in the hole diagonally above and to the right of the first one and come to the right

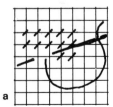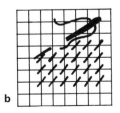

Illus. 5. Continental stitch. Always work right to left. Turn canvas upside down on even rows.

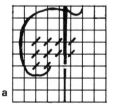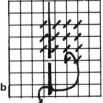

Illus. 6. Half Cross stitch. In a, a row is stitched left to right. In b, row is stitched right to left.

side again directly under the second hole; continue across the row this way. When you work a row from right to left, the needle points up rather than down (see Illus. 6).

Creative craftsmen like to personalize a piece that they buy with the design already worked. Most all of the designs you buy are worked in the Continental stitch and *Petit Point*, its smaller version. To make this doorstop a bit extraordinary, the background of the owl and mushroom design was made in the *Mosaic stitch*. This is a set of three diagonal stitches: short, long, and short, each set covering a 2 × 2 mesh box (that is, 2 vertical and 2 horizontal mesh). Follow Illus. 7 for this stitch. Work from the right to the left for continuous motion. Where the Mosaic stitch meets the design, just do as much of each set of three stitches as there is room for.

It is important that you plan the shape of the

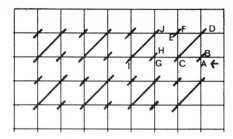

Illus. 7. Mosaic stitch. Follow the letters to see the stitching pattern.

area to be stitched before you begin. A covered brick uses only a certain area of a square canvas. Fold the sides of the canvas up around the brick and, with a waterproof marker, draw a line on the canvas where it touches the edges of the brick. Lay the canvas flat again and strengthen those lines, which are the boundaries of your stitching. The shape you stitch should be like that in Illus. 9.

Illus. 8. A detail of the doorstop shown in color on page 35. The Mosaic stitch background and Continental stitch design allow no threads of the canvas to show.

Blocking

The shape of your canvas will inevitably be slightly distorted once you have filled in the background, but you can restore the piece to its original shape by blocking it. Find a piece of scrap wood or insulation board a little larger than your needlepoint. (Insulation board is better because it allows a free circulation of air, so your needlepoint can dry quickly.) You also need a piece of paper the same size as the board to protect the canvas from stains, and either a staple gun or a large supply of pushpins for a border of blank canvas, or tacks for a finished edge.

Draw a 1″-grid—that is, a checkerboard pattern

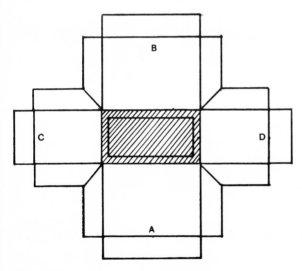

Illus. 9. The shape to be stitched for a brick doorstop. The shaded area represents the brick. Stitch an extra half inch around the marked area, as the canvas will shrink as you work on it.

—on the paper with a *waterproof* pen or marker and tape the paper to the board. Wet the needlepoint with a sponge dampened with cold water. (Hot water shrinks wool.) Place the needlepoint right side down on the board. Tugging gently, staple or tack one side of the margin *in a straight line.* Make sure that the corner is 90° and staple or tack the next side. Gently but firmly pull the other two sides into place, stapling as you proceed. The staples or tacks should be about $\frac{1}{2}″$ to $\frac{3}{4}″$ apart. Allow the needlepoint to dry thoroughly for two or three days. If the piece is still drastically out of shape after blocking, apply rabbit skin glue to the back. This glue can be bought in art supply stores. The principle of blocking is to reset the starch already on the canvas in the proper shape, so by adding rabbit skin glue you are just helping the regular process along.

Assembling

Find a solid brick with no chips or weak points which may crack. Pad the brick by wrapping a piece of foam rubber sheeting around it and glueing it there. Place the canvas face down on a table with the brick centered on top of it. Cut away the excess canvas in each corner, but not too closely to the stitching, since canvas ravels.

Fold sides A and B around the brick and whip them together with yarn. Turn up sides C and D, and stitch along the corners. Then whip the edges of sides C and D to each other. To cover the whipped stitches, glue a piece of felt to the bottom of the brick.

Lion and Tiger Pillows

A pair of animals makes complementary pillows for a den or other tailored room. The edges of the pillows on page 43 are covered with the *Scotch stitch*, different than the rest of the background, to make a border design. The Scotch stitch is a larger version of the Mosaic stitch, and covers a square of four mesh. This stitch has seven stitches, starting with a small one and growing larger until the middle diagonal stitch extends from one corner of the box to the other. Then the stitches grow smaller again until the box is completed. So that the ends of the rows are identical, begin the first row of the border in the middle and stitch toward the sides. Allow at least 1″- to 1½″-margin of blank canvas. Work from the right to the left, and turn the canvas when returning across a row.

For interest, vary the direction of every other stitch for the Reversed Scotch. The two rows on the outside are the same color as the rest of the background, and the next two border rows and the corners are a deeper color found in the design. The corners are worked according to the pattern in Illus. 12.

Put your initials and the date in one of the lower corners with the Continental stitch. (Refer

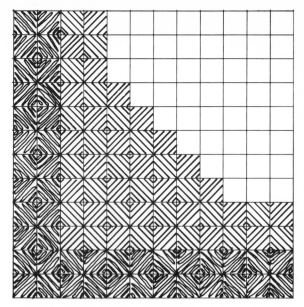

Illus. 12. Pattern for corner of pillows shown in color on page 43.

to the alphabet on page 4 for a stitching pattern of each letter. Each X represents one stitch.) The Continental is good for filling in designs and for detail. While it can be used as a background stitch, it usually distorts the canvas when used over a large area.

The *Basketweave stitch*, similar to the *Diagonal stitch*, fills in the background of these pillows. The stitch is not as good as the Continental for small areas, as it lacks maneuverability. A piece done with Basketweave has lots of give, or stretchability. You can stitch the Basketweave without turning the canvas around for return rows.

Begin the Basketweave stitch in the upper right corner of your piece and take two Continental

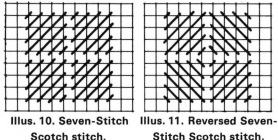

Illus. 10. Seven-Stitch Scotch stitch.   **Illus. 11. Reversed Seven-Stitch Scotch stitch.**

Illus. 13. Close-up of corner of tiger pillow. Stitch your name or initials in a corner with the Continental stitch, just as a painter signs his work.

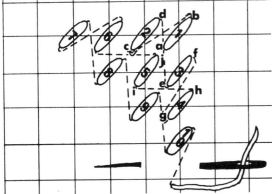

Illus. 14. Basketweave stitch. When you begin a new row at the top, make a Continental stitch to the left of the last stitch. When you begin a new row at the bottom, make a Continental stitch below the last stitch.

stitches (from right to left). Take a third stitch *under the first*, then a fourth stitch under the third, and the fifth and sixth diagonally above the fourth. Realize that you are stitching in diagonal rows, from the top to the bottom and the bottom to the top. The needle always goes beneath two mesh, from the area already worked to the area to be worked.

When you turn from a "down" row to an "up" row, the needle is horizontal on the wrong side. When changing from an "up" row to a "down" row, the needle is vertical on the wrong side.

Work two rows of Continental around the outside of the border in the same color as the last two border rows. These rows keep the blank canvas from showing when the pillow is put

11

together. After completing the stitching, block the needlepoint so it has square corners and straight edges.

The fabric you choose for the back of the pillow should harmonize with the needlepoint design in both color and texture, as well as with the room the pillow will be used in. For the rugged lion and tiger to be placed in a den, corduroy is an ideal choice. Pre-shrink the fabric by washing it in a machine and drying in the dryer. Measure the area of the worked needlepoint and to these measurements add $\frac{5}{8}''$ for seams all the way around. Mark this area on the backing material and cut the fabric.

Make cording with scraps of the backing. Attach the cording to the needlepoint piece so the stitching falls *just* outside the border of Scotch stitches. Place the right side of the backing fabric against the right side of the needlepoint and sew

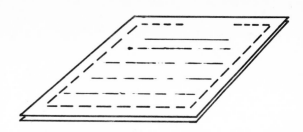

Illus. 15. Sewing canvas and backing fabric together. With right sides together, stitch around three sides and all four corners. Turn right side out and stuff.

three sides and all four corners on the sewing machine. Turn the pieces so the right sides face out, being sure to turn the corners completely. Stuff an inner-pillow, $\frac{1}{4}''$ larger on all sides than the needlepoint pillow cover, with shredded foam. Insert in cover and hand sew the fourth side.

Butterfly Picture

Making an Original Design

If you have searched the needlepoint shops for a challenging design but none seems quite right, you are probably ready to design your own pattern. Ideas for a design are endless: Children's coloring books are a good source for bold, simple shapes which you can fill in with fancy stitches. There are books on needlepoint at your library, and many of these have patterns that you can trace. A geometric pattern stitched in bold colors makes a striking accent, particularly in a contemporary home.

Sketch the subject on paper in the size you want the needlepoint piece to be. When you are satisfied with the lines of your drawing, go over them with a black felt tip pen. Place the proper canvas (see page 5) over the design. The canvas should be the size of the area to be stitched plus 2″ or 3″. Trace the design on the canvas with a *waterproof* felt tip pen. If you plan to use white or light yarn do not use black ink, as it shows through the yarn. Write the colors of each section on the original sketch and keep it nearby for reference.

Before you start stitching, bind the edges of the canvas with masking tape to prevent ravelling.

Keep the selvages—the closely woven sides of the canvas—on the sides of the needlepoint, not on the top and bottom.

Stitching

The butterfly on page 46 is a freehand design. Most of the stitches used are vertical, so Mono 14 canvas was chosen (that is, canvas woven with one strand, 14 mesh per inch). White is a better choice than ecru, because the bright yellow could be dulled by the darker color.

The black body of the butterfly is filled in with the *Brick stitch*, a simple vertical stitch over two mesh (see Illus. 16). Work in horizontal rows and skip every other mesh. When you stitch the second row, each stitch goes in the vertical row of mesh you skipped in the first row. Begin each stitch in the second row just one mesh below the line of mesh where the first row begins.

The black lines separating the colors on the wings are done in the Continental stitch. The *Parisian stitch* forms the larger yellow sections of the wings (see Illus. 17), and the rest of the wings are completed with vertical *Filling stitches*. Simply cover the canvas with one long vertical stitch to fill in the area between the black Continental stitches.

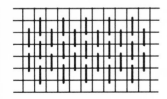

Illus. 16. Brick stitch.

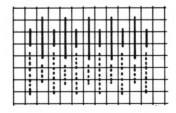

Illus. 17. Parisian stitch.

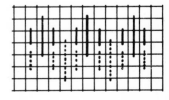

Illus. 18. Hungarian stitch.

13

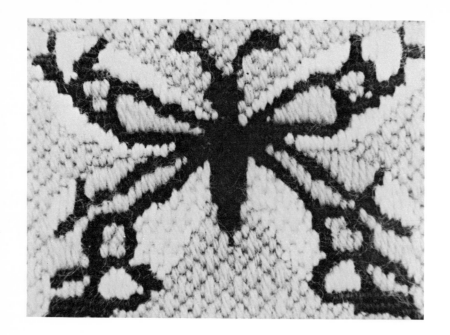

Illus. 19. Close-up view of butterfly shown in color on page 46. Background here is Hungarian stitch.

For a natural subject like a butterfly, a green background is a logical choice. The *Hungarian stitch*, a vertical stitch which looks like a diamond pattern, was used. It is based on three vertical stitches: work one stitch over two mesh, one over four, one over two, and skip a space. In the second row, place a short stitch under a short stitch, a long one in the space, and skip a space under the long stitch. The vertical columns are thus either all long or all short stitches.

Framing

When you have finished the stitching on your original design, block the piece as instructed on page 9. What you do with the needlepoint is as much up to you as the stitches and colors you use, but you might want to frame the piece. The butterfly on page 46 is surrounded by soft cork, a natural material that accents the beautiful colors of the insect.

Buy a piece of masonite or plywood the size you want both needlepoint and frame to be. Use white glue to attach the blocked needlepoint to the masonite. Cut out the center of a piece of heavy, dark brown cork, or cut four separate strips to surround the stitchery. The cork must be even with both the edges of the masonite and the edges of the stitching so no blank canvas shows.

Eyeglass Case

Needlepoint items are not limited to home decorations. The man in your life will enjoy showing off a hand-made needlepoint eyeglass case with his initials on it. Even if he doesn't wear prescription lenses, he still needs a case for sunglasses!

With all the new shapes in lenses and frames, standard measurements no longer apply. Measure the particular glasses that the case is to fit to determine the area of canvas you need. For the case on page 46, Penelope 10 canvas was chosen. Allow five mesh ($\frac{1}{2}''$ of canvas) on all sides for a hem, and one mesh at the fold line. There are two ways of constructing the eyeglass case, shown in Illus. 20. The width of scraps you have determines which layout you should use.

The first stitches you make should be the initials. Decide where they are to be and work them in the Continental stitch. Refer to the alphabet on page 4.

Fold the five-mesh hem to the wrong side. Line up the holes and baste the hem in place with

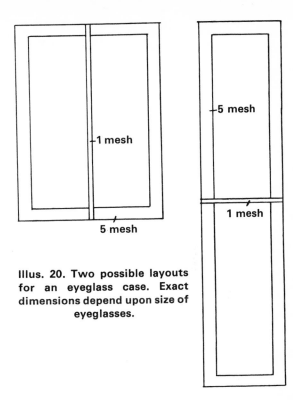

Illus. 20. Two possible layouts for an eyeglass case. Exact dimensions depend upon size of eyeglasses.

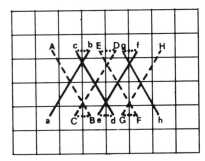

Illus. 21. Two-Color Herringbone stitch requires two trips across the canvas.

heavy carpet thread. When you stitch over this hem, work as if it were one thickness. The edge will be one mesh of canvas, and you cover it with the *Binding stitch* (see below).

Work the border next in the *Two-Color Herringbone stitch*. Stitch from the left to the right only. Beginning in the upper left mesh that you want to cover, take a diagonal stitch down 3 mesh and to the right 2 mesh (that is, 3 × 2). Bring the needle out again one mesh to the left in the same row. Take a 3 × 2 diagonal stitch up and to the right, and bring the needle out one mesh to the

15

left in the same row. Continue around the edge of the canvas. For the second color, begin three mesh directly below the start of the first stitch. Take a 3 × 2 stitch up and to the right. Continue as for first color.

The background is worked in the *Jo-Jo stitch* (Illus. 22), which creates a diamond effect but is made with horizontal and vertical stitches. It resembles the Reversed Scotch stitch (page 10) which uses diagonal stitches. Start at one side of the case and when you meet an initial, do only as much of the stitch as you have room to stitch. Continue on the other side of the initial as if you had used the Jo-Jo stitch straight across. Continue with the Jo-Jo stitch on the back of the case, or use another stitch in this book.

When there is no margin of blank canvas on

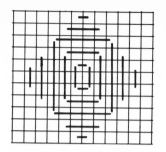

Illus. 22. Jo-Jo stitch creates a textured background as the stitches change direction.

the edge of the stitching, as is the case here, use copper tacks instead of staples to hold the needlepoint while you block it. Staples cut the wool, but tacks do not leave marks.

To protect the lenses of the eyeglasses, line the

Illus. 23. Stitch right up to an initial with the Jo-Jo stitch; then continue on the other side as if you had stitched straight across. See page 46 for the completed eyeglass case.

16

canvas with a soft fabric. Instead of sewing it to the canvas, use one of the new products that allows you to bond the fabric to the canvas by ironing (Stitch Witchery by Dritz, for example). Follow the directions that accompany the product.

To put the eyeglass case together, use the Binding stitch. Begin stitching along the fold and move to the right, following Illus. 24 as you read these instructions. Secure the thread by taking one stitch in each of the first two holes from the back to the front. Skip one hole and go into the fourth hole from the back to the front. Go into the second hole from the back; then go into the fifth hole from the back. From the fifth, go into the third, then sixth, fourth, etc. Notice that you are skipping one space when you travel backward, and going into the next empty space when travelling forward. Always bring the wool over the edge and always go into the back of the canvas. The stitch looks like a neat braid along all the sides of the eyeglass case.

When you are finished assembling the case, spray it with a waterproofing product to protect it from dirt, dust, and stains. In spite of the pre-

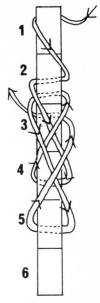

Illus. 24. The Binding stitch looks intricate, but once you get the knack, it goes quickly. Each number represents one hole of the canvas.

cautions you take to keep the piece clean, it will someday need a thorough cleaning. Send it to a professional dry cleaner. Tell him that the fibre content is wool, and he will clean and treat it properly.

Footstool

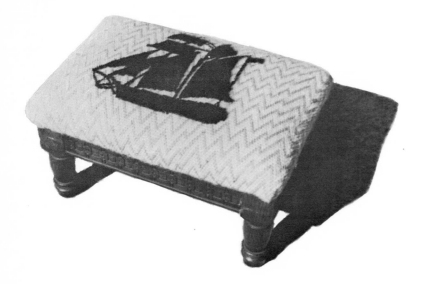

An excellent example of combining another interest with needlepoint is shown in the footstool in Illus. 25. The designer is obviously fond of ships! The room that this footstool was designed for is decorated with a sailing and whaling theme. Simple designs such as this ship look striking when solidly stitched as a silhouette, and almost any stitch and combination of colors works well as the background of a silhouette. The ship was stitched in the Brick stitch, and the background in the popular *Bargello stitch*. Because these are vertical stitches, the canvas chosen is Mono 14.

The three similar colors in the background resemble waves, which are appropriate to the design.

Here the Bargello stitch was worked over four mesh, but any number mesh is possible with this straight stitch. See Illus. 26 and 27 for the background diagram. Begin the background in the middle of the canvas and work to the sides for a balanced pattern.

If you plan to use the needlepoint piece to cover a footstool, as this ship was used, be sure the canvas is large enough to tuck around the edges of the top of the stool. Have a professional upholster the footstool, as it is a job involving a lot of know-how. When the cover gets dirty, have it cleaned by a professional dry cleaner for the best results.

18

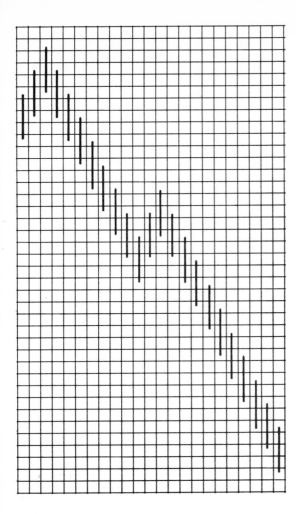

Illus. 26. Some of the background of the foot-stool uses this stitching pattern. Each line represents one Bargello stitch. When you finish the canvas, spray it with a waterproofing product.

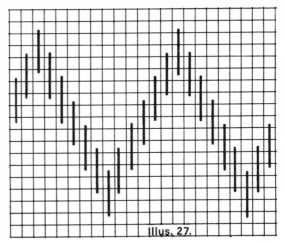

Illus. 27.

Illus. 28. The footstool fits right into this nautical room. Ships in bottles on the wall, scrimshaw and other ornaments connected with sailing continue the theme.

Quickpoint Pillow

Quickpoint is simply needlepoint on large Penelope canvas with four or five mesh to the inch. This is also called rug canvas. Penelope 5 is usually used for vertical stitching, and Penelope 4 for diagonal stitching. Use a size 13 needle.

The pillow in color on page 42 was done in quickpoint. It looks like a *sampler*—a canvas on which you practice a variety of decorative stitches—but actually it was carefully planned for both color and stitching. Penelope 4 canvas and yarn made especially for it were used. It is also possible to make this pillow with two strands of tapestry yarn on Penelope 5 canvas.

Decide on the size you want the finished pillow to be and add 2″ of canvas to each side for a margin. Cut a canvas this size and tape the edges so the threads do not ravel. Divide the stitching area into nine squares (three across by three down). Separate the squares by working the Half Cross stitch between them (see page 7). When you work a row from right to left, the needle points

down as it comes to the right side. When you work a row from left to right, the needle points *up*. The thread is diagonal on the right side, vertical on the wrong side.

The pillow in Illus. 64 is covered with a variety of diagonal stitches. Bright colors are next to cool ones, and simple stitches are next to more intricate ones. Begin your pillow by stitching your name and the date in one corner in the Continental stitch. After separating the squares with Half Cross stitches, you are ready to fill in each square with a different color and stitch. Try some of those that the pillow in Illus. 64 uses:

Milanese stitch: The Milanese stitch is a set of four diagonal stitches that form a triangle covering half a square 4 mesh × 4 mesh. The diagonal stitches are over 1, 2, 3 and 4 mesh. Each row of stitches is a diagonal row. In the second row, the triangles point in the opposite direction. The smallest stitch of the second row is worked in the same mesh as the longest stitch of the first row.

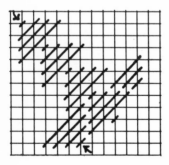

Illus. 29. Milanese stitch.

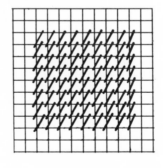

Illus. 30. Interlocking Gobelin stitch.

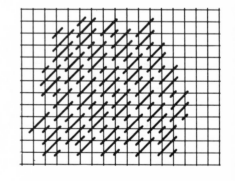

Illus. 31. Diagonal Cashmere stitch.

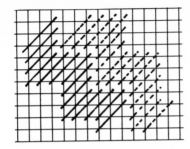

Illus. 32. Byzantine stitch.

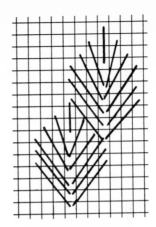

Illus. 33. Leaf stitch.

Interlocking Gobelin stitch: Work the first row just like a row of Half Cross stitches, but make each stitch diagonally over two mesh by one mesh (2 × 1). The tops of the stitches in the second row are one mesh above the bottoms in the first. Be careful that you do not split the yarn in the stitches that have already been worked. For better backing, you can work this stitch like the Continental rather than the Half Cross stitch.

Diagonal Cashmere stitch: Start at the top left corner of the area to be worked and travel diagonally downward and to the right. Each Diagonal Cashmere stitch is composed of three stitches, one short (over one mesh) and two long (over two mesh). In the second row the first long stitch is diagonally below the short stitch of the first row.

Byzantine stitch: The Byzantine stitch looks like a staircase: the rows are worked in sets of four diagonal stitches, each 3 × 3. There are four stitches down and four stitches across for each step.

Work this like the Continental for a good background.

Leaf stitch: The Leaf stitch is a set of five pairs of diagonal stitches plus one vertical stitch. Each stitch begins one mesh above the beginning of the preceding stitch. The first three pairs of stitches are 4 × 3; the fourth pair is 4 × 2; the fifth pair is 4 × 1. The vertical stitch is 3 mesh tall. The second row of Leaf stitches fits between the stitches in the first row. The vertical stitch of a Leaf stitch in the second row begins one mesh below the top of the bottom stitch of a Leaf stitch in the first row.

Use some stitches you have already learned, like the Mosaic and Scotch stitches. When you have completed the stitching, block and assemble the pillow as instructed on page 12.

21

Bolero

The bolero on page 47 was done in the versatile *Bargello stitch*. This stitch is rapidly becoming a popular needlepoint stitch because of the many different effects that can be achieved with it. You used the Bargello stitch exclusively in the background of the footstool (page 18); in this bolero, you again use just the Bargello stitch, but the effect is more colorful than before.

Choose a prepared pattern for a vest. Press the tissue pattern pieces with a cool iron and lay them flat on a table. Tape the side seams of the front and back together. Trace the pattern on Mono 14 canvas, turning the pattern at the center of the back to draw the other half of the bolero. Draw in the stitching lines (dotted lines) and the darts with a *waterproof* marker.

Work the Bargello stitch according to the sketch in Illus. 35. Start in the center of the back and work to the front to balance the pattern. To work the center of a large canvas, roll the excess. Stitch into two mesh on the canvas you allowed for the seam allowance at the shoulders, and into two mesh on the center of the darts. Block the canvas before you assemble it.

With your sewing machine, make zig-zag stitching around all the edges where the stitching ends to prevent ravelling. Cut off any excess canvas, leaving a $\frac{1}{4}''$-seam. Sew the darts and shoulder seams on the sewing machine. Cut the lining from a lightweight lining fabric, according to the same pattern. Sew the darts, shoulder and side seams of the lining on the sewing machine.

With the wrong sides together, baste the lining and the needlepoint around the outside edges. Bind these edges by stitching a braided edging to the needlepoint on the sewing machine. Finish the bolero by attaching a button-and-chain closing.

Illus. 34. Detail of bolero (shown in color on page 47). Bargello stitch makes this wavy pattern.

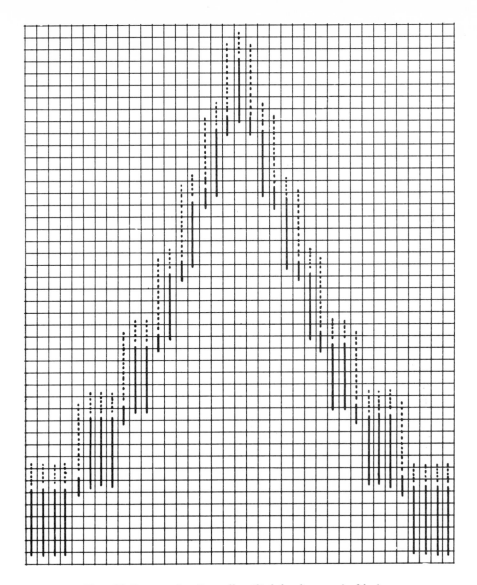

Illus. 35. Pattern for Bargello stitch background of bolero.

Mushrooms

Decorative stitches add depth to your needle-point designs. They are a lot more interesting than the plain Half Cross and Continental stitches that are so popular, and because they break up solid areas of stitching, you cover the canvas much faster than with plain stitches. Some of them suggest certain details—flowers, insects, stars—by virtue of their design. Once you learn these stitches, planning an original design will be easy.

Plan your piece down to every last detail before you begin. The colors might determine the stitches you use, and the stitches definitely determine the canvas you use. The mushroom piece in Illus. 40 has a large variety of stitches and colors, so white Penelope 10 canvas was used—its versatility allows almost any stitch to be made on it. The mushroom design was traced on the canvas from an original sketch, and the color and stitch key was written on the sketch and used as a guide.

Stitches Resembling Flowers

Star stitch: The Star stitch covers a square 4 × 4. It is made up of eight stitches, each two mesh wide, all going into the center mesh. Make the four stitches which form the upright cross first. A *French knot* in a contrasting color accents the center. To make one, wrap the yarn around the needle three times and insert the needle into the canvas.

Triple Leviathan stitch: The diagonal stitches cover a square 4 × 4. There are 12 separate diagonal stitches, all going into the center. The upright crosses (2 × 2) touch each other. The entire stitch needs an area 6 × 6.

Medallion stitch: This is a very visual stitch and it is best done by following the sketch. One hint: make the small upright cross in the center last. The Medallion stitch covers a square 8 × 8.

Ray stitch: The Ray stitch covers a square 3 × 3.

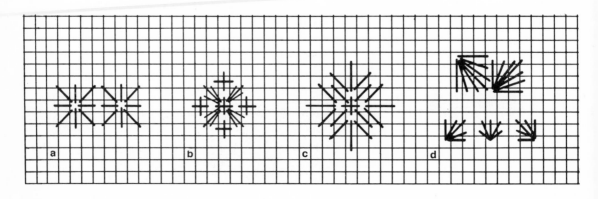

Illus. 36. In <u>a</u>, Star stitch; <u>b</u>, Triple Leviathan stitch; <u>c</u>, Medallion stitch; <u>d</u>, Ray stitch and variations.

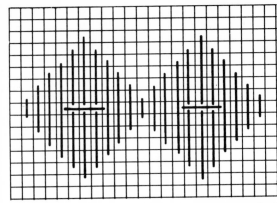

Illus. 37. Dormstadt Pattern. Center vertical stitches break in the middle and are only six mesh long.

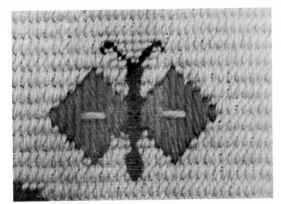

Illus. 38. Close-up of insect (color on page 26). Short stitch in middle of Dormstadt Pattern is replaced by body of French stitches.

All of the seven stitches extend from one mesh. The stitches may be turned any way for certain effects. For flower buds in the mushroom design, Ray stitches are upside down on a 2 × 2 square with only five stitches instead of seven.

Improvise an Insect

The *Dormstadt Pattern* is a logical design for an insect. This is a series of vertical stitches over an even number of mesh in a diamond pattern: 2, 4, 6, then two sets of 5, 6, 5 over each other, then 6, 4, 2. The horizontal stitch extends over four mesh. Use a contrasting color for interest.

Instead of the center short stitch of the Dormstadt Pattern, the *French stitch* runs between the two diamonds for the body of the insect. Three motifs, placed one on top of the other, form the sectional body of an insect. Each French stitch is a set of two vertical stitches, four mesh tall, placed between one pair of vertical mesh. Each vertical

stitch is tied down to the adjacent vertical mesh with a horizontal stitch over one mesh.

The *Three Stitch Cross* (3 × 2) makes a good-sized head for our insect. The antennae are done in *Petit Point*, which is a miniature version of the Continental stitch. When the two threads of the Penelope 10 canvas are separated, there are 20 mesh to the inch. Penelope 10 is sometimes called Penelope 10/20 because of this. Split the threads of Penelope canvas apart and stitch with

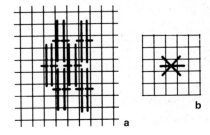

Illus. 39. In a, French stitch; b, Three Stitch Cross.

Illus. 40. Bright, lively and fresh, mushrooms done in textured needlepoint stitches can add color to any wall in your home. If you frame the canvas, do not cover it with glass, as this hides the texture.

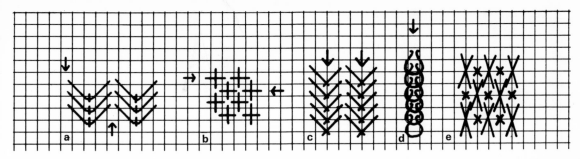

Illus. 41. In <u>a</u>, Stem stitch; <u>b</u>, Upright Cross stitch; <u>c</u>, Fern stitch; <u>d</u>, Chain stitch; <u>e</u>, Double stitch.

two plies of a 4-ply tapestry yarn. Four Petit Point stitches cover the same area as one Continental stitch. It is necessary to do small items in Petit Point for detail. The snail in the lower left corner of the mushroom piece is a good example of Petit Point, as are the name and date.

Mushroom Stems

Stem stitch: From the upper left corner, take a 2 × 2 diagonal stitch down and to the right. Make the second stitch directly below the first. Continue to make a column the desired length. The second column consists of 2 × 2 diagonal stitches which slant up and to the right. Make a vertical back stitch between each column.

Upright Cross stitch: The Upright Cross is two perpendicular stitches which are two mesh high and two mesh wide. The second row fits between the crosses of the first row.

Fern stitch: Work this stitch from the top to the bottom only. Take a 2 × 2 diagonal stitch down and to the right. Bring the needle up one mesh to the left on the same row. Take a 2 × 2 diagonal stitch upward and to the right. The

second stitch begins one mesh below the mesh where the first stitch began. This stitch makes a fat, neat braid.

Mushroom Caps

Chain stitch: Work the stitch from the top of the chain to the bottom. It makes a vertical row of loops that are stitched down between two mesh. Hold the canvas so that you work horizontally from right to left. Bring the needle out of the canvas and loop the yarn to the left. Insert the needle into the canvas in the same hole you came out of, while you hold the yarn loop with your left thumb. Bring the needle up on the same horizontal row, two mesh to the left, inside the loop. Pull the yarn gently but firmly. Repeat the instructions to the end of the row. To begin another row, cut the yarn and begin again at the right.

Double stitch: The Double stitch is a combination of the Cross stitch and the Oblong Cross. The Oblong Cross is 3 × 1 and the Cross is 1 × 1. The Oblong Cross shares holes with the

27

Illus. 42. The lower right corner of mushrooms (color on page 26). Shown are Woven Scotch, Fern, Continental, Slanted Gobelin, Star, Ray and Reversed Scotch stitches.

Crosses directly above and below it.

Diagonal Cashmere stitch: (page 20–21).

Continental was used for the cap of the yellow mushroom, and scattered *Smyrna Crosses* give a polka dot look. This is an Upright Cross on top of a regular Cross. It covers a 2 × 2 square and makes a bumpy stitch.

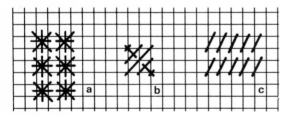

Illus. 43. In <u>a</u>, Smyrna Crosses; <u>b</u>, Woven Scotch stitch; <u>c</u>, Slanted Gobelin.

A similar technique forms the mushroom on the lower right. A background of Five-Stitch Scotch stitches has squares of *Woven Scotch stitches* scattered across the cap. To make a Woven Scotch, stitch a box of Five-Stitch Scotch and then weave a second color over and under those stitches.

Finishing

The border is a combination of several stitches: from the inside out, there is one row of Continental, two of Reversed Five-Stitch Scotch, one of regular Five-Stitch Scotch, and two of Continental added so no canvas shows when the piece is framed.

The background is filled in with *Slanted Gobelin.* This is a diagonal stitch, 2 × 1, which is usually worked like the Half Cross. It may be

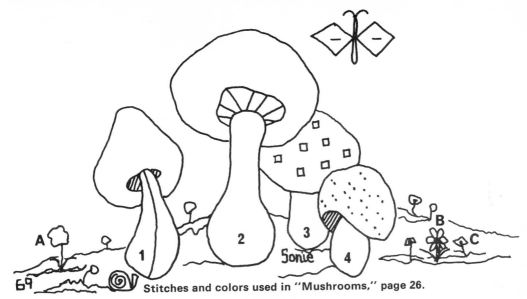

Stitches and colors used in "Mushrooms," page 26.

Mushrooms

Cap

1. orange, burnt orange
   Double stitch
2. wine red
   Diagonal Cashmere stitch
3. Spanish gold, green
   Continental, Smyrna Cross
4. burnt orange, white
   Five-Stitch Scotch and Woven
   Scotch stitches

Flowers
A. red, Triple Leviathan stitch
B. shocking pink, Medallion stitch
C. shocking pink, Star stitch, with grape
French knot
Remaining flowers: red, yellow, shocking pink
variation of Ray stitch
Grass: two shades of green Continental stitch
Snail: wine red and green Petit Point
Sky: sky blue Slanted Gobelin stitch
Signature: red Petit Point

Underside

1. burnt orange
   Continental stitch
2. gold, wine red
   Continental, Chain stitches
3. ——
4. wine red
   Continental stitch

Insect
wings: orange and yellow Dormstadt Pattern
body: wine red French stitch
head: wine red Three Stitch Cross
antennae: wine red Petit Point
Border
one row brown Continental stitch
two rows green Reversed Five-Stitch Scotch
stitch
one row dark green Five-Stitch Scotch stitch
two rows dark green Continental stitch

Stem

1. two shades of beige
   Continental stitch
2. brown
   Stem stitch
3. yellow
   Upright Cross stitch
4. pink
   Fern stitch

29

Illus. 44. Close-up of background and top of orange/burnt orange mushroom. This section, turned on its side, also appears on the cover. Shown are Slanted Gobelin and Double stitches, and border of Continental and Reversed Five-Stitch Scotch stitches.

made like Continental to provide a better backing. The grass and flower stems in two shades of green are worked in Continental.

Because there is so much texture, you should block a piece like this with its right side out, to prevent flattening these stitches. Use this piece any place you would use needlepoint (see page 5 for ideas)—but after so much planning and detailed stitching, you probably want it to last a long time. Have it framed by a professional for best, longest-lasting results.

Illus. 45. Detail of mushrooms showing snail and date in Petit Point, grass in Continental stitch and flower in Triple Leviathan.

Illus. 46 and 47. Searching for a new idea for your needlepoint? Have your youngster color a pleasing scene. Plan your stitches and colors according to this picture and then stitch! Follow the irregular lines of the original drawing for an interesting design.

Cat Wall Hanging

To immortalize a memory, scene or cherished possession, transfer a likeness of the subject to canvas and fill it in with simple stitches for a unique, personal design. If your subject is very detailed or you are trying to portray an exact likeness, merely tracing your design on canvas will not give the desired detail. The cats in the wall hanging on page 34 were carefully charted on graph paper (see sketch in Illus. 50). Each square represents one mesh of the canvas, and various symbols represent different colors. Use graph paper which is the same size as the canvas—here,

Illus. 48. Background of Milanese stitch and border of Ray and Four-Trip Herringbone stitches in cat wall hanging (page 34).

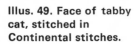

Illus. 49. Face of tabby cat, stitched in Continental stitches.

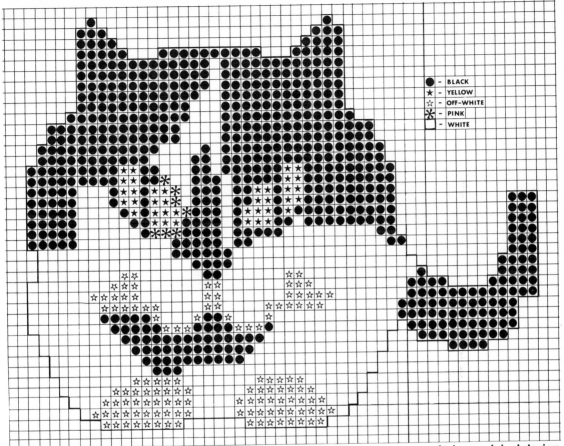

Color key:
- ● – BLACK
- ★ – YELLOW
- ☆ – OFF-WHITE
- ✳ – PINK
- □ – WHITE

Illus. 50. Diagram for the middle cat, Pepper, on page 34. When you want to stitch an original design, plan every hole of the canvas as carefully as this before you even thread the needle.

both paper and canvas have five squares to the inch (reduced here to fit on the page).

While you must use the Continental stitch for the design, the background may be almost any stitch. This hanging uses the Milanese stitch, a fast stitch good for filling in large areas.

Turn the hem under as you did on the eyeglass case (page 15) and stitch the border through both thicknesses. The border here is divided into two sections: the top and bottom, and the sides, for a frame-like appearance. Two rows of the Ray stitch edge the top, bottom and corners. The

33

second row of Ray stitches points in the opposite direction from the first. The sides are edged with two rows of *Four-Trip Herringbone*. This is worked in the same way as Two-Color Herringbone, but each stitch here is 3 × 3. It takes four trips to cover the canvas completely instead of two.

Work the Binding stitch all around the edges for a finished look. Attach clip-on curtain hooks to the top of the hanging, and hang the piece from a dowel rod that you have stained, antiqued, or painted. Finish the ends of the rod with decorative drawer knobs.

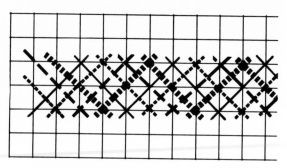

Illus. 52. Four-Trip Herringbone stitch.

Illus. 51. If you chart the design carefully, your finished needlepoint piece inevitably looks realistic.

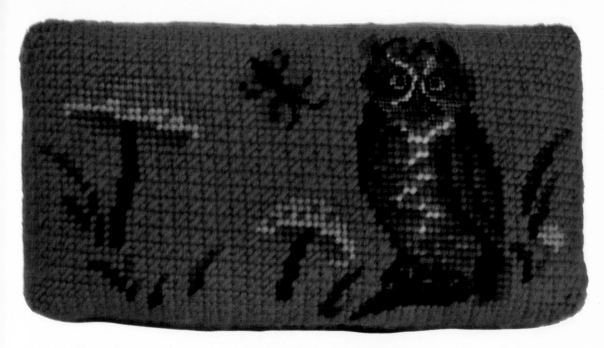

Illus. 53. The owl and mushroom doorstop, described on page 7, uses bright colors to give a gay note to a usually drab furnishing.

Rooster

Craft, needlework, and women's magazines offer many ideas for needlepoint projects. These designs can easily be enlarged or reduced to the proper size by the *grid method*. This method was used to enlarge the rooster on page 38, and you can use it with the sketch of the rooster or any other drawing you want to make up in needlepoint.

Draw a $\frac{1}{4}''$-grid over the design to be enlarged. On another piece of paper draw a $1''$-grid with the same number of squares. Copy the portion of the drawing in each of the small squares in the corresponding large squares. By using these dimensions, you will increase the size of the original design four times, and by changing the size of both grids, you can vary the size of your final design. Simply reverse the process to reduce the size.

Once the drawing is the proper size, trace it on the canvas. Mono 12 canvas was used for the rooster because it is easy to see while working on it, and because a large number of stitches can be made on it.

As in the mushroom project, this rooster was made with many different stitches for texture and to make the stitching itself more interesting and faster to do. Shading creates a varied look also, and can be effectively used to break up a solid

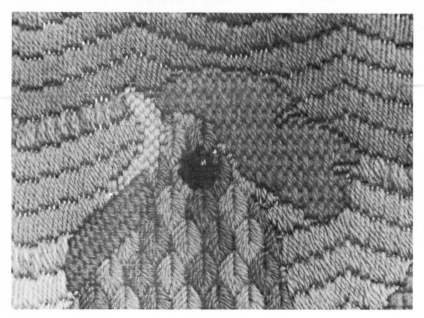

Illus. 54. Detail of rooster (color on page 38), showing shaded background and rooster's head. Bright spot in center of eye is metallic thread.

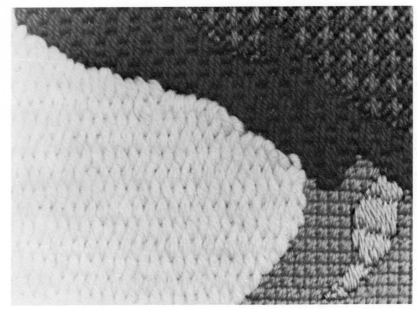

Illus. 55. The light area here is the sun, stitched in the Plaited Gobelin, of the rooster design. Darker areas are sections of the rooster.

background area. In the rooster project, the sky is lighter near the rising sun and darker farther away. To achieve this effect, split four-ply yarn of one color and combine some of its strands with those of another color. The sky closest to the sun is stitched with four strands of light blue (color A). The next section uses three strands of A and one of a darker shade of blue (color B); then two of A and two of B; then one of A and three of B; and, finally, four strands of B. The procedure begins again with three strands of B and one of an even darker blue (color C), and then two strands and two strands, one and three, and four of color C. Combine darker shades until you reach the color you want.

Even though the magazine from which you took the project suggests simple stitches, you should be able to use the knowledge you have gained here to make a more interesting and textured design. Many stitches used in the other projects are repeated here—Bargello, Brick, Parisian, Leaf, Hungarian, Mosaic, Scotch, Interlocking Gobelin, Byzantine, Diagonal Cashmere, and Slanted Gobelin—as well as many new stitches:

Plaited Gobelin: All the stitches are 4 × 2, and each stitch is two mesh away from the one next to it. The second row begins two mesh above the bottom of the first row and slants in the opposite direction. Thicken your yarn to cover the canvas by using two strands from a four-ply yarn that

37

Illus. 56. Bright beyond belief, the rooster crows his approval of his colors and stitches. While the colors on his body are related, the tail feathers burst forth with vibrant contrasts.

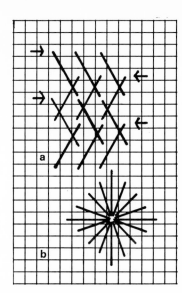

Illus. 57. In **a**, Plaited Gobelin; **b**, Diamond Eyelet stitch.

Illus. 58. A decoration for a Christmas tree illustrates the use of metallic thread for sparkle.

you have split, with a full four-ply yarn. The sun was filled in with this stitch.

Diamond Eyelet stitch: The entire stitch covers a square 8 × 8. It is made up of 16 separate stitches, each going into the center. Stitch the four longest stitches that form the upright cross first, each one over four mesh. A Diamond Eyelet makes the rooster's eye. A few Continental stitches were taken in the center of the Diamond Eyelet with a metallic yarn.

NOTE: On wall hangings only, you may stitch small areas with scraps of weak knitting worsted. Novelty and textured yarns, such as mohair, angora, straw, nylon and metallic, may also be used for special effects. Remember that these do

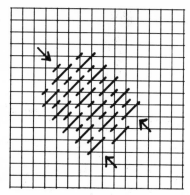

Illus. 59. Diagonal Mosaic stitch.

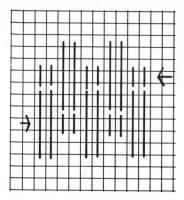

Illus. 60. Old Florentine stitch.

not have enough strength for items which will receive a lot of wear.

Diagonal Mosaic stitch: Make a series of alternating short and long stitches in a diagonal row. Begin either at the top or at the bottom. The diagonal lines running opposite to the direction of the rows alternate short and long stitches.

Old Florentine stitch: A row of Old Florentine stitches consists of pairs of vertical stitches alternating in length: first two stitches two mesh long, then two stitches six mesh long. The tall stitches go over the short ones in subsequent rows.

Oblique Slav stitch: Oblique Slav is a diagonal stitch 2 × 4. There are two mesh between the start of each stitch and each row. The stitch slants to the right and is worked like the Half Cross.

Diagonal Scotch stitch: Work boxes of the Scotch stitch diagonally, and share the end short stitch with the next box. For subsequent rows, the shortest stitch is diagonally below the longest stitch.

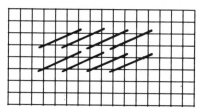

Illus. 61. Oblique Slav stitch.

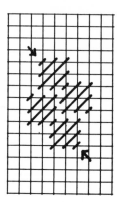

Illus. 62. Diagonal Scotch stitch.

40

Illus. 63. Stitches used in Rooster, page 38

1. Brick
2. Diamond Eyelet
3. Parisian
4. Diagonal Mosaic
5. Leaf
6. Old Florentine
7. Hungarian
8. Pattern Darning
9. Scotch
10. Interlocking Gobelin
11. Greek

12. Byzantine
13. Oblique
14. Cashmere
15. Milanese
16. Diagonal Scotch
17. Diagonal Cashmere
18. Slanted Gobelin
19. Mosaic
Sun — Plaited Gobelin
Background — Bargello

Illus. 64. A quickpoint pillow is covered with a variety of stitches. Their different textures show up well because of the loose canvas and thick yarn that are used in quickpoint.

Illus. 65. Another quickpoint pillow using different stitches and colors. A pair of these livens up a somber den or casual living room.

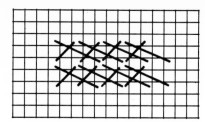

Illus. 66. Greek stitch.

Greek stitch: Actually a Cross stitch with one short arm and one long arm, each Greek stitch is intertwined with the next one. Work from the left to the right only. The first stitch is a 2 × 2 diagonal upward and to the right. Bring the needle up in the same row two mesh to the left. Make a 4 × 2 diagonal downward and to the right. Bring the needle up two mesh to the left in the same row. Repeat the instructions to the end of the row, and start the second row directly below the first. The short stitches of one row touch those in the second, as do the long stitches in each row.

Illus. 67. Lion and tiger pillows, described on page 10, are not as colorful as Quickpoint Pillows. Instead, these creatures add a quiet dignity to a room, in keeping with their revered position in the animal kingdom.

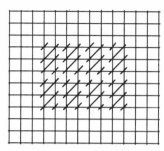

Illus. 68. Cashmere stitch.

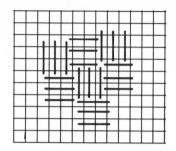

Illus. 69. Pattern Darning.

Cashmere stitch: A set of four diagonal stitches, this stitch covers a 3 × 2 rectangle. Stitch in a continuous motion right to left or top to bottom. The short stitches are over one mesh, the long ones over two.

Pattern Darning: This stitch is a combination of three horizontal and three vertical stitches, each stitch over three mesh. The stitches alternate to form a checkerboard pattern.

Illus. 70.Top feather of the rooster's tail was done in the Scotch stitch. Sections below are Interlocking Gobelin and, to the right, Greek stitch. Below is Byzantine stitch.

Illus. 71. Close-up of base of rooster's tail feathers. See sketch in Illus. 63 for exact position relating to entire rooster.

The border of the rooster wall hanging, is edged the same way as the border of the cat wall hanging (see page 35), and this piece is also hung from a dowel. If you want to copy this piece exactly, enlarge the sketch in Illus. 63 and use the stitches indicated. By now, however, you should be able to design your own patterns, plan interesting colors and decorative stitches, and, in general, be creative!

Illus. 72. Another section of the rooster's tail, beginning with the area numbered 11 (see Illus. 63).

Illus. 73. An eyeglass case can be made using small scraps of canvas leftover from other projects. For an inexpensive yet thoughtful gift, personalize a case with the recipient's initials. Directions are on page 15.

Illus. 74. This bright butterfly, described on page 13, has been framed with soft cork. It makes an attractive wall decoration for a sunny room.

Illus. 75. Also framed in cork, this wise owl stares hauntingly at the viewer.

Illus. 76. A lively bolero (see page 22 for instructions) tops any outfit with color and style. When you cut the canvas to the tissue paper pattern, pay attention to which pattern lines are for cutting and which are for seams. This is important, as it affects the fit of your bolero!

Index